At least our bombs
are getting smarter

D1359872

At least our bombs are getting smarter

a cartoon preview of the 1990's by **TOLES**

PROMETHEUS BOOKS
BUFFALO, NEW YORK

Published 1991 by Prometheus Books

with editorial offices at 700 East Amherst Street, Buffalo, New York 14215-1674, (716) 837-2475; and distribution facilities at 59 John Glenn Drive, Amherst, New York 14228-2197, (716) 691-0133

95 94 93 92 91   5 4 3 2 1

Library of Congress Cataloging-in-Publication Data

Toles, Tom.
    At least our bombs are getting smarter : a cartoon preview of the 1990's / by Tom Toles.
        p.   cm.
    ISBN 0-87975-709-4 (alk. paper)
    1. United States—Politics and government—1989-   —Caricatures and cartoons. 2. United States—Politics and government—1981–1989—Caricatures and cartoons. 3. American wit and humor, Pictorial. I. Title.
E881.T65   1991
973.928'0207—dc20   91-19793
                                                                                                            CIP

Printed on acid-free paper in the United States of America

Introduction

Someone once said
that drawing a daily
editorial cartoon is like
holding a gun that
never stops firing. I
think it was me.

Tom Toles

PSYCHIC PREDICTIONS

FOR THE 1990'S

1990	1991	1992	1993	1994
 CATCHING THE SPIRIT OF THE BERLIN WALL, HOLLAND OPENS ITS DIKE.	 THE SUPREME COURT REAFFIRMS CONSTITUTIONAL RIGHT TO ABORTION AFTER THE FIRST $30,000 IN INCOME.	 BUSH DECLARES HE WILL BE THE EDUCATION PRESIDENT.	 WEST GERMANY PUTS BERLIN WALL BACK UP TO KEEP EAST GERMANS OUT.	 LITHUANIA SENDS TANKS INTO MOSCOW TO KEEP RUSSIA FROM DROPPING OUT OF THE SOVIET UNION.
1995	1996	1997	1998	1999
WASHINGTON DC BECOMES 51ST STATE.	QUAYLE DECLARES HE WILL BE THE EDUCATION PRESIDENT.	 UNITED STATES BECOMES 47TH PREFECTURE OF JAPAN.	 TELEVISION STILL THE ONLY ADDICTIVE DRUG LEGAL FOR CHILDREN.	 GOVERNMENT LEADERS PROMISE ENVIRONMENT WILL BECOME A SERIOUS ISSUE ANY TIME NOW. NEXT MILLENIUM FOR SURE!

 TOLES UNIVERSAL PRESS SYND. ©1989 THE BUFFALO NEWS

December 31, 1989

7

January 12, 1989

January 17, 1989

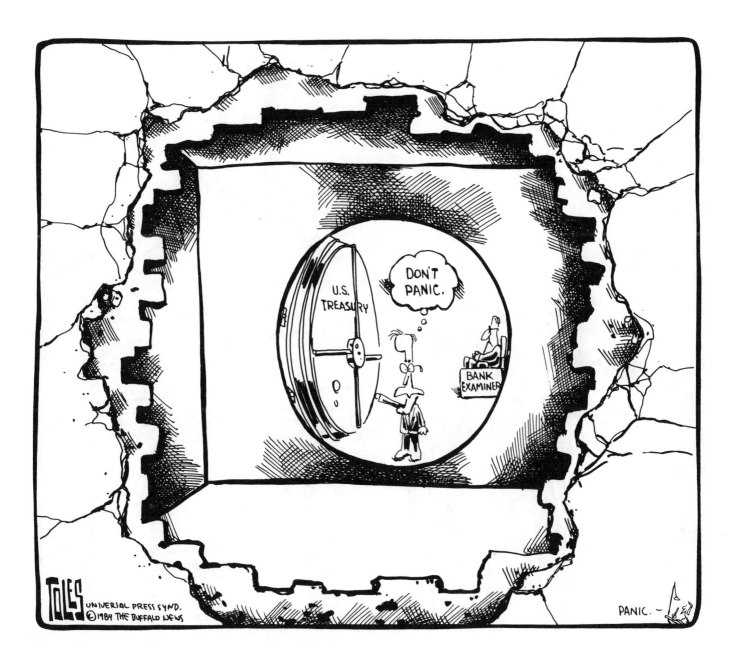

George Bush: The First 100 Minutes

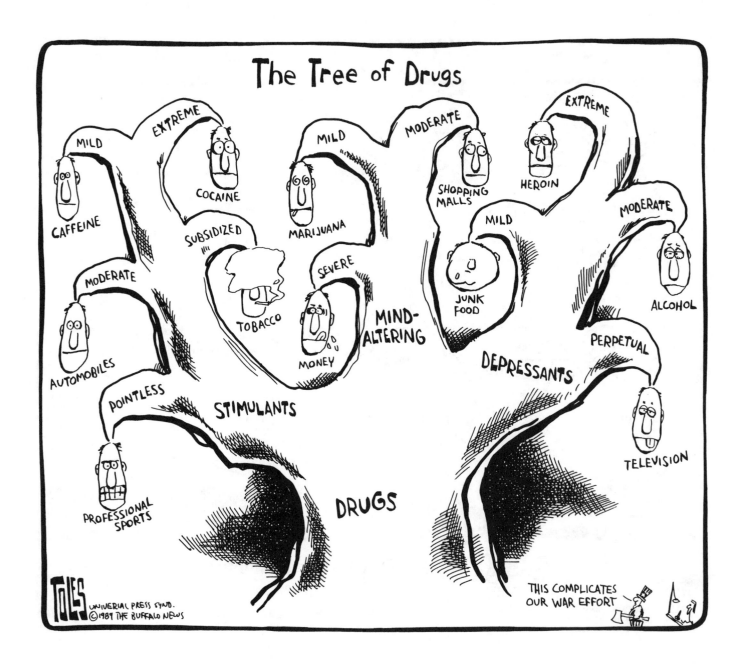

February 27, 1989

16

April 13, 1989

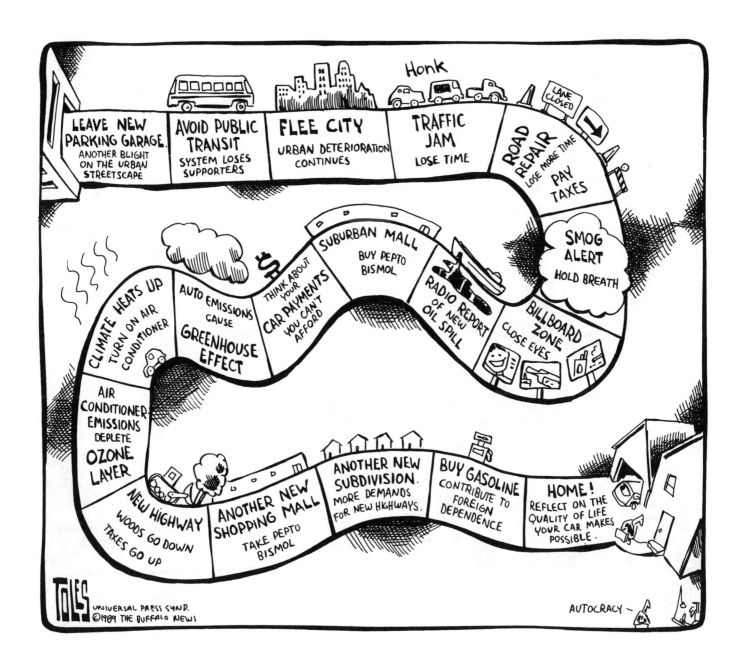

April 23, 1989

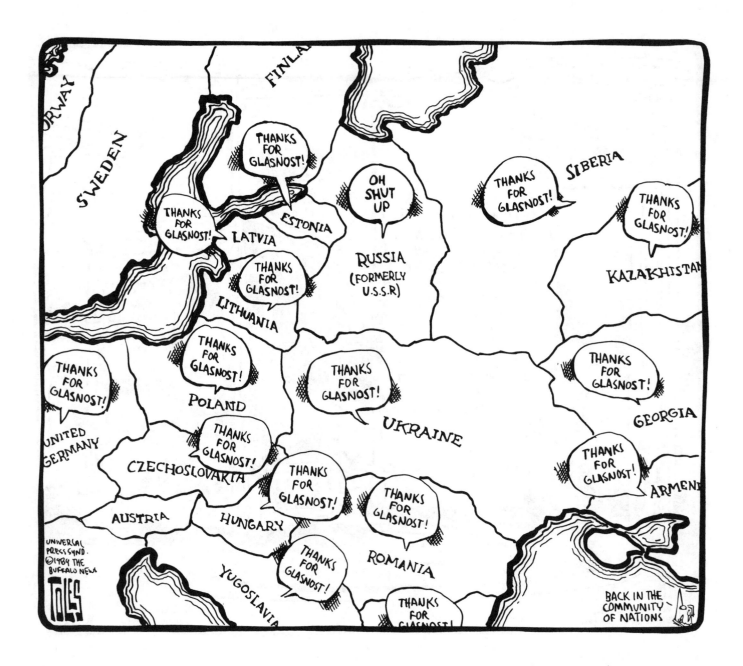

June 14, 1989

June 19, 1989

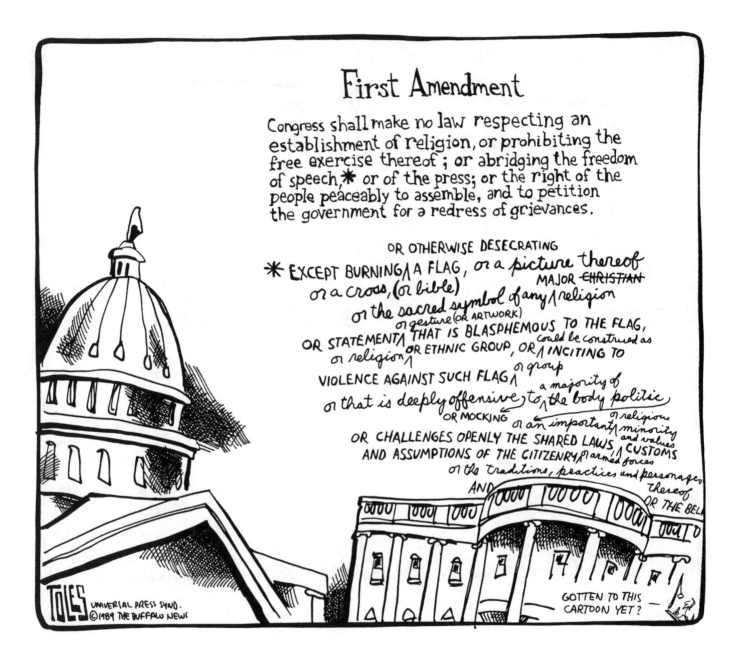

First Amendment

Congress shall make no law respecting an establishment of religion, or prohibiting the free exercise thereof ; or abridging the freedom of speech,✳ or of the press; or the right of the people peaceably to assemble, and to petition the government for a redress of grievances.

✳ EXCEPT BURNING⟨ᴏʀ ᴏᴛʜᴇʀᴡɪsᴇ ᴅᴇsᴇᴄʀᴀᴛɪɴɢ⟩ A FLAG, or a picture thereof or a cross, (or bible) MAJOR ~~CHRISTIAN~~ or the sacred symbol of any⟨religion or gesture (or ARTWORK)⟩ OR STATEMENT⟨THAT IS BLASPHEMOUS TO THE FLAG, or religion⟩OR ETHNIC GROUP, OR⟨could be construed as⟩INCITING TO VIOLENCE AGAINST SUCH FLAG⟨or group⟩ or that is deeply offensive⟨a majority of⟩to⟨the body politic⟩ OR MOCKING or an important⟨or religion minority and values⟩ OR CHALLENGES OPENLY THE SHARED LAWS⟨CUSTOMS⟩ AND ASSUMPTIONS OF THE CITIZENRY⟨armed forces⟩ or the traditions, practices and personages AND thereof OR THE BEL

TOLES
UNIVERSAL PRESS SYND.
©1989 THE BUFFALO NEWS

GOTTEN TO THIS CARTOON YET?

July 25, 1989

This cartoon not funded by the National Endowment for the Arts

UNIVERSAL PRESS SYND.
©1989 THE BUFFALO NEWS

I THINK THE ARTIST HAS CAPTURED SOMETHING... — STOP IT!

August 6, 1989

August 8, 1989

August 10, 1989

DO YOU REALIZE...

THAT IF WE GET AN AGREEMENT ON TROOP REDUCTIONS

SHORT-RANGE MISSILES

TANKS

FIGHTER PLANES

HELICOPTERS

ANTI-AIRCRAFT GUNS

LONG-RANGE MISSILES

SUBMARINES

BATTLESHIPS

AIRCRAFT CARRIERS

BOMBERS

CHEMICAL WEAPONS

MOBILE MISSILES

SPACE DEFENSES

BAZOOKAS

CANNONS

UNIVERSAL PRESS SYND. ©1989 THE BUFFALO NEWS

TOLES

SERVICE REVOLVERS

AND BAYONNETS,

REDUCING OUR OVERALL DEFENSE BUDGET MAY EVEN BE POSSIBLE.

—THEORETICALLY.

August 15, 1989

Look at me, look at me,
Look at me now.
It all can be done
But you have to know how.

I can hold new elections
When there's nothing to eat,
I can hold off the public's
Demands for some meat.

I can juggle republics
As simple as that.
But that is not all,
Said the cat in the hat

I can get rid of Stalin,
I can publish new books,
I can cut short-range missiles
Despite dirty looks.

I can do all of this
While I hop on a ball,
But that is not all,
No, that is not all........

DON'T TURN
THE PAGE!

August 27, 1989

If you've been playing for an hour and don't know who the patsy is, you're the patsy.

THEY SAID THEY'LL LEND ME MONEY UNTIL MY LUCK CHANGES!

TOLES
UNIVERSAL PRESS SYND.
© 1989 THE BUFFALO NEWS

September 15, 1989

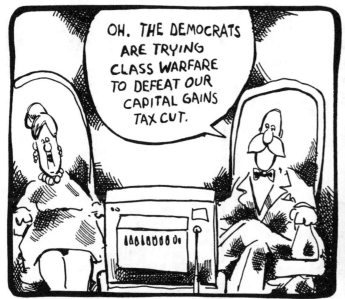

40

October 23, 1989

December 13, 1989

THE GARBAGE BARGE RONALD REAGAN JUNK BONDS AYATOLLAH KHOMEINI STAR WARS
EORGE BUSH DAN QUAYLE DENG XIAOPING JIM BAKKER TAMMY BAKKER JESSICA HAH
ORAL ROBERTS PAT ROBERTSON WALTER MONDALE GARY HART DONNA RICE JIM WRIGH
TONY COELHO ED MEESE FEDERAL DEFICIT STOCK MARKET CRASH IVAN BOESKY RADON
CHAEL MILKEN DONALD TRUMP FRANK LORENZO CORPORATE TAKEOVERS TRADE DEFICI
UPREME COURT VALDEZ OIL SPILL CHERNOBYL COLD FUSION SAVINGS AND LOAN CRISI
MOAMMAR GADHAFI MANUEL NOR ANIEL ORTEGA NICOLAE CEAUSESCU
MICHAEL DUKAKIS OZONE H ANCY REAGAN DONALD REGAN T
ANCY REAGAN'S ASTROLOGE ALCOLM FORBES' PARTY PW B
SYLVESTER STALLONE SA ZSA GABOR STEALTH BON
COCAINE CRACK ICE MX MISSILE ACID RAIN F
YITZHAK SHAMIR B JESSE HELMS JESSE JACKSO
JIMMY THE GREEK CARAGUA EL SALVADOR
ASPAR WEINBERGER OBERT BORK PETE ROSE
VANNA WHITE RIO LYN NOFZIGER YUPPIES
ERNARD GOETZ A IRLINE SAFETY HOMELESSN
ALEXANDER HAIG B EAGAN PRESS CONFERENCES
NUCLEAR WASTE STOR RAINFOREST DESTRUCTION T
LEBANON MICHAEL DEAVE NDON LAROUCHE LEE IACOCCA
KURT WALDHEIM BHOPA GRAMM-RUDMAN LEE ATWATER
ERDINAND MARCOS IMELDA MARCO AL SHARPTON PLASTIC PACKAGING
OLIVER NORTH FAWN HALL ADMIRAL POINDEXTER WILLIAM CASEY LOUIS FARRAKHAN
EPUBLICAN PARTY DEMOCRATIC PARTY CAPITAL GAINS TAX CUT AIRLINE TERRORISM SA
CAMBODIA AFGHANISTAN TIBET RADIO MARTI CHEMICAL WEAPONS JOHN HINCKLEY NUC
CREATIONISM APARTHEID JERRY FALLWELL 1982 RECESSION JEANNE KIRKPATRICK COLD WA
DAVID STOCKMAN DAN RATHER YURI ANDROPOV KONSTANTIN CHERNENKO LEON
CANDIDATE DEBATES STATE PRIMARIES TV CAMPAIGNING

I SURVIVED THE 1980's

CLIP OUT AND ATTACH TO FOREHEAD WITH A LARGE THUMB TACK AND HEAVY RUBBER MALLET

TOLES
UNIVERSAL PRESS SYND.
©1990 THE BUFFALO NEWS

48

February 23, 1990

1985: GENERAL SECRETARY

OF THE SOVIET UNION, EASTERN EUROPE, AND A WORLDWIDE COLONIAL EMPIRE

1988: PRESIDENT

OF THE SOVIET UNION AND THE POLISH INSURRECTION

1990: SUPER-PRESIDENT

OF RUSSIA AND THE INNER SOVIET REPUBLICS

©1990 THE BUFFALO NEWS
UNIVERSAL PRESS SYND.

TOLES

1994: GRAND MAXIMUM EMPEROR-IN-CHIEF POTENTATE SUPREME

OF DOWNTOWN MOSCOW

A POOH-BAH'S HOME IS HIS CASTLE

March 1, 1990

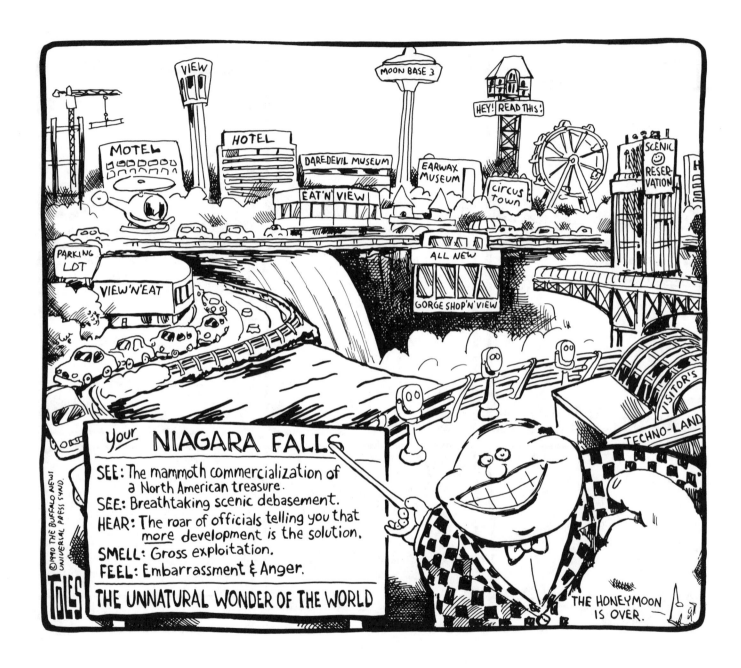

March 27, 1990

PROPOSED NATURE PARK

PARKING LOT

HOTEL

CONVENTION, BANQUET FACILITIES

VIEWING TOWER/ REVOLVING RESTAURANT

INFORMATION

SIDEWALK

SHOPPING COMPLEX

FOUNTAIN COURT

INTERPRETIVE CENTER/ MOVIE THEATER

REST ROOMS

PAVED VIEWING AREA

NATURE

CONCESSIONS

FOOD COURT

SOUVENIRS

TOLES

UNIVERSAL PRESS SYND.
©1990 THE BUFFALO NEWS

ANYWHERE, U.S.A.

April 16, 1990

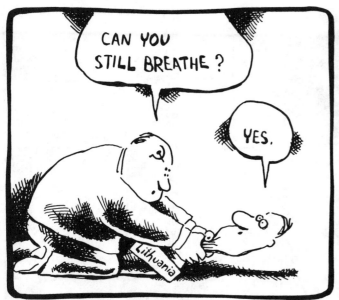
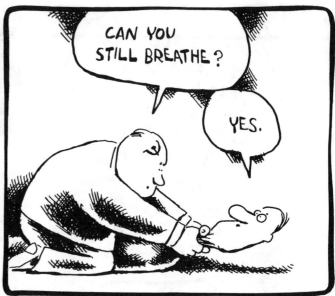
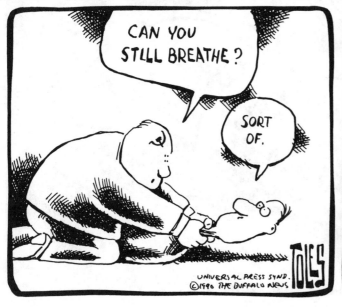

April 18, 1990

May 6, 1990

A compromise: "It shall be an offense to attack, damage, deface, burn, kick or step on an American flag except one that a politician has wrapped himself in."

Toles

UNIVERSAL PRESS SYND.
S ©1990 THE BUFFALO NEWS

TORO!

May 17, 1990

May 27, 1990

May 28, 1990

June 19, 1990

July 3, 1990

72

August 15, 1990

The General and the Mrs.

YOU HAVE TO UNDERSTAND SADDAM HUSSEIN IS HITLER.

THEN WHY DID WE USED TO SUPPORT HIM?

THAT WAS WHEN HE WAS ATTACKING KHOMEINI, AN EVEN BIGGER HITLER.

I THOUGHT GADHAFI WAS HITLER.

HE'S ALREADY HAD HIS 15 MINUTES AS HITLER.

LIKE YASSER ARAFAT?

HE WAS HITLER UNTIL ABU ABBAS TOOK OVER AS HITLER.

WHERE DOES THAT LEAVE SYRIA'S ASSAD?

HE CAN BE HITLER AGAIN AFTER WE TAKE OUT SADDAM.

TOLES
UNIVERSAL PRESS SYND.
©1990 THE BUFFALO NEWS

LOT OF HITLERS.

WE'RE FRESH OUT OF STALINS.

...UNTIL POL POT GETS BACK IN

DIDN'T WE USED TO SUPPORT HIM?

August 21, 1990

Another Hostage Situation

September 17, 1990

September 19, 1990

September 24, 1990

October 9, 1990

October 18, 1990

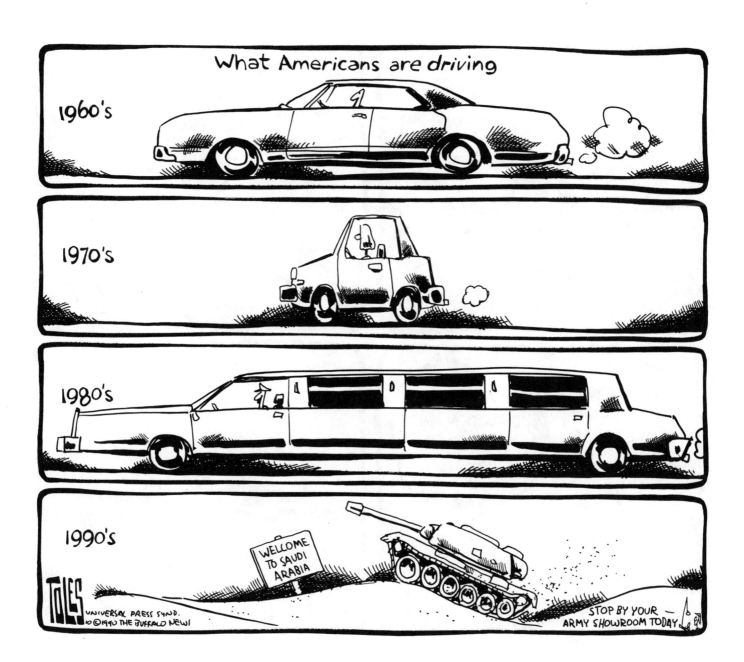

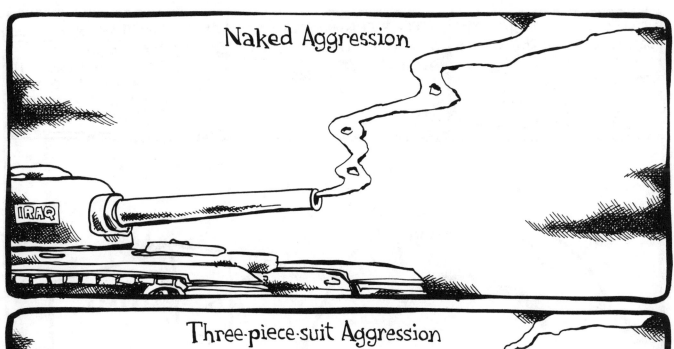

November 6, 1990

November 14, 1990

98

November 19, 1990

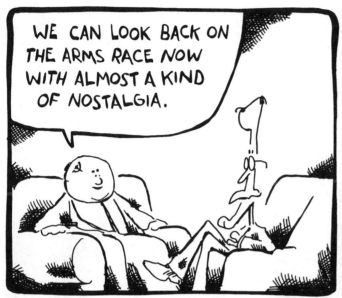

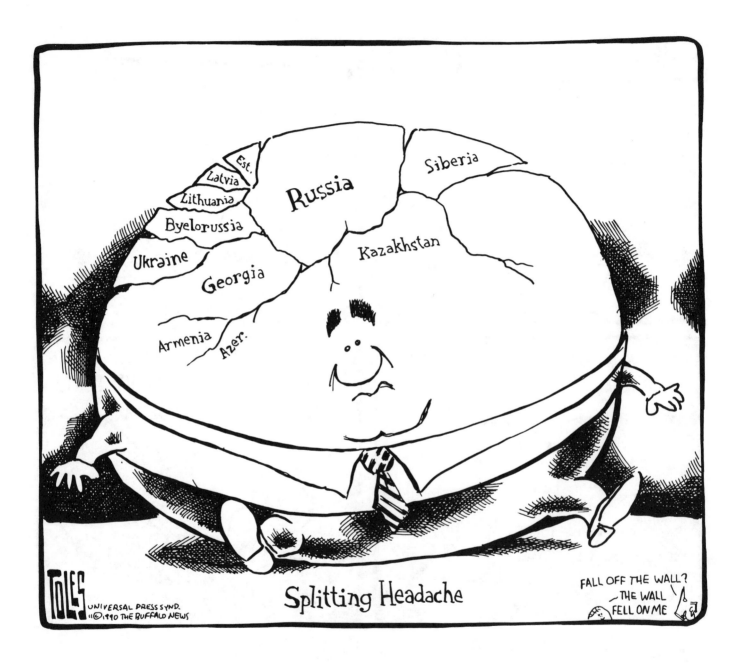

Splitting Headache

Foxes guarding the fox den

January 8, 1991

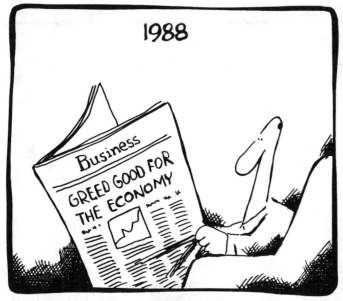

1988

1989

1990

We learned our lesson.

1991

January 20, 1991

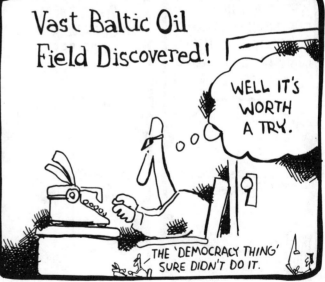

YES IT WAS WORTH SPENDING ALL THAT MONEY ON HIGH-TECH WEAPONS!

WATCH THEM KNOCK OUR HEALTH-CARE CRISIS OUT OF THE AIR!

SEE THEM GO RIGHT DOWN THIS SMOKESTACK AND SAVE OUR ENVIRONMENT!

WATCH THEM SEEK OUT AND CATCH THE $500 BILLION S&L THIEVES WHERE THEY HIDE!

SEE THEM BLOW OUR HIGHEST-INFANT-MORTALITY-IN-THE-INDUSTRIALIZED-WORLD RIGHT OUT OF THE WATER!

TOLES UNIVERSAL PRESS SYND. ©1990 THE BUFFALO NEWS

WATCH THEM TARGET AND WIPE OUT WIDESPREAD ILLITERACY!

SEE THEM VAPORIZE THE THREE TRILLION DOLLAR NATIONAL DEBT THAT YOU AND I OWE!

WATCH THEM SOLVE THE UNDERLYING CAUSES OF CENTURIES-OLD MIDEAST CONFLICT!

WELL, OKAY, THEY CAN'T DO EVERYTHING.

BUT WATCH THEM FIX OUR INFRASTRUCTURE!...

January 28, 1991

February 17, 1991

SHOULD HAVE KEPT GOING RIGHT INTO BAGHDAD.

AND PUT A DEMOCRACY IN THERE.

THEN KEEP RIGHT ON GOING INTO IRAN.

THEY COULD USE A BIT OF DEMOCRACY TOO.

THEN TAKE CARE OF SYRIA, JORDAN AND THE OCCUPIED TERRITORIES.

PUSH ACROSS INTO EGYPT AND LIBYA.

THEN SWING AROUND BACK INTO SAUDI ARABIA.

TOLES

A LITTLE DEMOCRACY WOULDN'T HURT THEM ANY.

DID I LEAVE ANYBODY OUT?

JUST KUWAIT.

OH YEAH

March 5, 1991

March 7, 1991

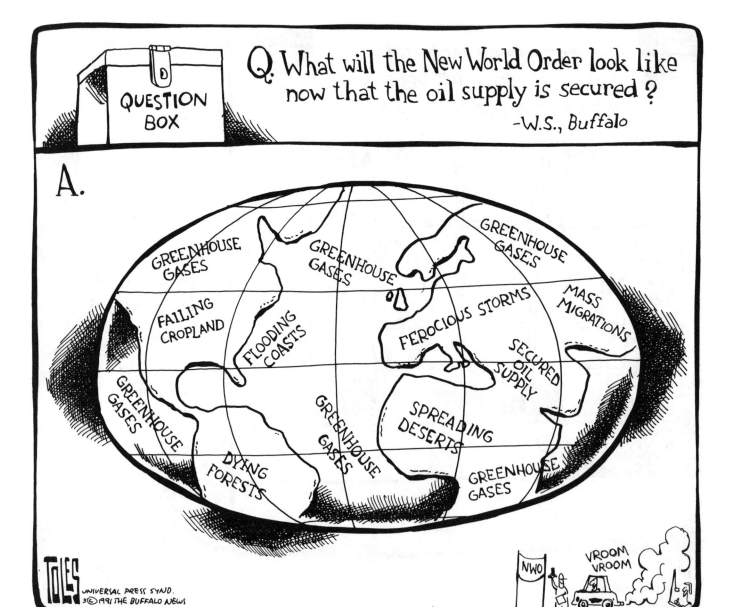

March 12, 1991

March 19, 1991

HERE'S THE LA POLICE BEATING VIDEOTAPE AGAIN...

...BIGFOOT TRUCK CRUSHES ALL OTHERS!...

..."RAZOR BABYSITTER" COMING TO A THEATER NEAR YOU...

...WRESTLEMANIA!...

...LAURA PALMER'S OWN FATHER MURDERED HER...

...ALLIED FORCES CARPETBOMBED THE HAPLESS IRAQI DRAFTEES...

...FOOTBALL!...

3©1991 THE BUFFALO NEWS/UNIVERSAL PRESS SYND.

TOLES

...HERE'S THE LA POLICE BEATING VIDEOTAPE AGAIN...

...OFFICIALS EXPRESS OUTRAGE...

?

POOR VIDEO QUALITY?

March 24, 1991

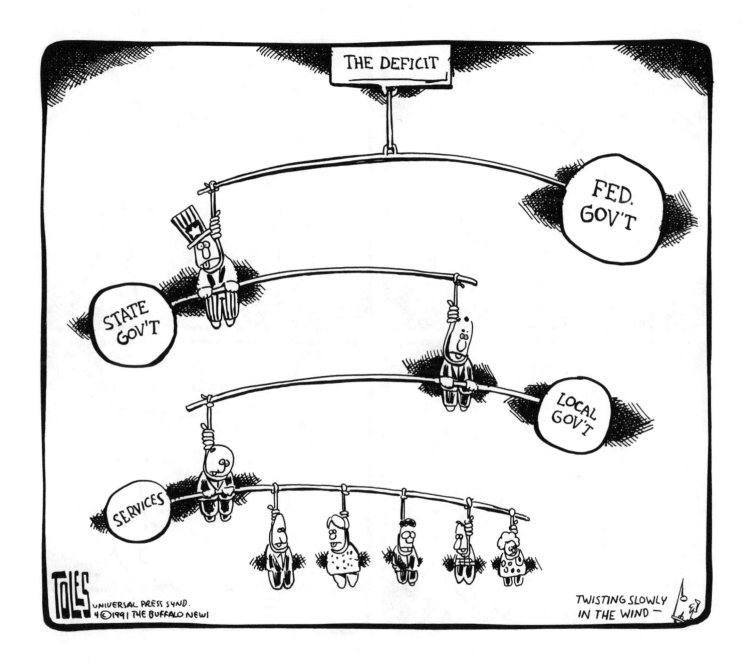

April 9, 1991

IT'S TIME TO INSURE ISRAEL'S LONG-RANGE SECURITY.

MUBARAK

AND TIME TO STOP OUR WEST BANK SETTLEMENTS AND GIVE THE PALESTINIANS A HOMELAND.

SHAMIR

AND END THE INTIFADA AND BEGIN AN ERA OF TRUE ARAB-ISRAELI PEACE.

ARAFAT

AND ESTABLISH A STANDARD OF DEMOCRACY THROUGHOUT THE REGION.

ASSAD

TOLES
UNIVERSAL PRESS SYND.
4 ©1991 THE BUFFALO NEWS

I'D SAY WE'RE MAKING REAL PROGRESS HERE.

BUSH

I'D SAY THIS IS ONLY A CARTOON.

MODERATOR

RIGHT?

April 22, 1991